for Sue Alex

THE NAMES OF THE SEA-TROUT

with best wishes
from

Tom Rawling
6 September
1993

THE NAMES
OF THE
SEA-TROUT

Tom Rawling

Tom Rawling

Littlewood Arc

Published by Littlewood Arc
Nanholme Mill, Shaw Wood Road,
Todmorden, Lancs. OL14 6DA

Design by Tony Ward
Printed by Arc & Throstle Press
Nanholme Mill, Todmorden, Lancs.
Typeset by Anne Lister Typesetting
Beacon Business Centre, Halifax.

ISBN 0 946407 87 8

Acknowledgements are due to the
editors of the following magazines
where some of these poems have
previously appeared: *Anglo Welsh
Review, New Poetry 6 Arts Council
Anthology, The Countryman, The Green
Book, The Honest Ulsterman, Lancaster
Festival, Lines Review, Literary Review,
Mandeville Bestiary, The Observer, Other
Poetry, Outposts, Oxford Poetry, Poetry
Book Society Anthology 1989 and 1991,
Poetry Durham, Poetry Review, Poetry
Wales, Rialto, Verse.* Also from *Ghosts at
my Back* (OUP, 1982), *A Sort of Killing,*
(Old Fire Station Poets, Oxford, 1978) and
The Old Showfield, (Taxus Press, 1984).
'Privy' was shortlisted in the Observer
Arvon Competition, 1985.

The author wishes to thank the
Hawthornden Trust for the fellowship
enjoyed in 1986 at Hawthornden
Castle.

The publishers acknowledge financial
assistance from Yorkshire and
Humberside Arts Board, North West
Arts Board and Southern Arts.

*For my daughters
Sue and Jane,
and for Pauline and Anne,
steadfast friends*

CONTENTS

I
The Names of the Sea-trout / 9
Torridge Salmon / 10
A Shared Rod / 11
Fisherman to Salmon / 12
Leviathan / 13
Crossing to Fish / 14
Night Fisherman / 15
Moonrise / 16
Alder-tree / 17
Feathers / 18
Acid Rain / 20
March Blackbirds / 21
Sea-gulls / 22
Black Dogs / 23
Ants / 24
Hedgehog / 25
Sheep-dog and Shepherd / 26
Wicks / 27
Firethorn / 28
Sloe Gin / 29
Midwinter / 30
On your Farm / 31
Clipping Day / 32
Hearthwords / 34
Rootcutter / 35
The Eel / 36

II
The Barn /39
Wild Strawberries / 43
Three Flowers / 44
Lesser Celandines / 46
Let Me Go / 47
Privy / 48
Scar / 50
Cold Tea / 51
Rumbutter / 52

When Stones Went Wild / 53
Not in a Silent Void / 54
Rams' Heads / 55
Grandmother / 56
Lake District National Park / 58
Bruce's Cave / 60
Sutton Hoo Burial / 61
Sutton Hoo Shoulder-Clasp / 62
Rosslyn Chapel / 63
About the Author / 64

I

THE NAMES OF THE SEA—TROUT

He who would seek her in the clear stream,
Let him go softly, as in a dream,
He who would hold her well,
Let him first whisper the spell
Of her names,

The silver one, the shimmering maiden,
The milkwhite-throated bride,
The treasure-bringer from the sea,
Leaper of weirs, hurdler to the hills,
The returning native, egg-carrier,
The buxom lass, the wary one,
The filly that shies from a moving shadow,
The darter-away, the restless shiner,
Lurker in alder roots,
The fearful maid,

Night dancer, ring maker,
The one that splinters reflections,
The splasher, the jester, the teaser, the mocker,
The false encourager, tweaker of lures,
The girl who is fasting, destroyer of hopes,
Bender of steel, the breaker, the smasher,
The strong wench, the cartwheeler,
The curve of the world.
She who doesn't want to surrender,
The desired, the sweet one.

When you've spent nights and days
Speaking her names, learning her ways,
Take down your tackle from the shelf,
And your skill. She may give herself
For the whispered spell.

TORRIDGE SALMON

for Hugh Falkus and Ted Hughes

Soft light through cloud,
the dark-ale river brimming its banks,
a March hayfield overhead in the purpled alders.
And more jetsam of last week's spate,
an ash-tree complete, tossed out on the beach,
sprawling its forty feet, live swelling buds.
Young willow bark blushing into flame

by Island Run. There she might lie
under the streaming froth
she'd tasted down in Bideford Bay
and known no choice, only the urge
to leap and run against the flood,
seek out her natal gravel,
make it her bridal bed.

First searching casts self-conscious
until the head forgot to try,
let the body flow into the rod.
Then the line unrolled its loop,
the lure reached where the eyes looked,
swam slow past her window.
A petition was offered,
again and again.

Gentle, with soft-mouthing surprise,
with a gleam unexpectedly golden
deep in the stained pool,
she came for the feather
found the hook.
What followed was the craft of killing.
Her virgin scales cling to my hands.

A SHARED ROD

Most days a Fabergé flash, the shock
of his being there then gone
in swift evasion, but today
the kingfisher doesn't jink,
he heads for the reeds that hide me.
My bamboo rod-tip skips,
lightning perches, horse-chestnut fire,
he is fish-scale peacock dazzle.

I hold my breath. I could touch him.

His wedge head swivels, searching,
the rod a bridge between us.
Will he plunge, explode with a beakful?
His great eye turns, a moment's stare,
then, blue-green whirr,
the arrow skims downstream,
leaving an emptied space,
a shared rod quivering.

FISHERMAN TO SALMON

Audacious your odyssey,
Salmo the Leaper;

You were so near your redd,
Your shrunken gut
Forbade all feeding,
Urged you to ripen;

But you came to my lure,
Betrayed yourself
For a feather.

LEVIATHAN

All day, thunder and the weight of rain,
white manes steeple-chasing down
Red Beck, running raw with haematite.

All day I waited till the rainbow came
to reassure my mother, then splashed
towards the chorus of the spate.

By a swollen gutter-end, a raft
of hay was swirling, I crouched to plop
my bait across drowned knapweed,

watched where the line pierced,
fingertips aching for a trout's tug,
but knew I had come too late.

When, a depth-charge hump erupted
into spray into arc into something
surf-riding for frozen seconds,

till the tackle snapped.
Only a field from home, I'd waded
into mystery, tampered with Leviathan.

CROSSING TO FISH

Above the mark of the highest tide,
where mud and marsh become hard rock
clean grass on gravel,
the first ford up the dale
made itself for men to find.

safe crossing now for swinging udders,
tractors bouncing under bales of hay —
sometime, a killing ground.

The Prince's men no longer bonny,
harried in this narrow valley,
blood oozing in the stream.

Harness-jingling Muncaster lords,
cold-eyed, falcon-wristed,
hoof-spray chasing Norman game.

Roman helmets out from Hardknott
send scouts forward, interlock their shields
against an ambush here.

Wild men come round Raven Crag,
wade slash and stab,
drive salmon to the reddening shore.

The swing-bridge creaks beside the ford,
worn boards beneath my feet,
a swaying path not air not ground,
and in the wavering dusk
old water voices lift and fall.

NIGHT FISHERMAN

I come at dusk to the dub
where sea-trout rest,
let the day slide behind the ridge,
wait by the dry-stone wall
till the distant bank advances.
I hear an old ewe's husky cough,
the water slopping slapping,
but listen, taut
for the important interjection
of a lunging fish.

Lips taste the mist of falling dew,
the tang of trodden nettles
cuts through the milkiness of cows,
earth's body-scent floods in.
Skin opens to the night, unlocks another
sense first recognised in youth,
found then from further back,
before books, before words.
The body pulses
with the valley's beat,
absorbing and absorbed,
moves when the moment comes.

Boots remember boulders, where to turn
half-left, then right, a steep step down,
a trodden path, the ancient track.
Now touch is master, blindman fingering
of reel and rod, the hook's keen point.
Feet shuffle-feel the ground,
delicately crunch the gravel,
body poised ready to reach
beneath the mirror of the pool,
hands in time with the flexing
spring of built bamboo, the back-cast
pulling, storing power
for the forward drive,
the lure's leap.

MOONRISE

Through darkness thicker than shadows,
the land lulled for predators,
my feet nudge the path to the pool.
I hear the splash of big fish
know they will come to my lure,
and for half an hour they do.
Then there is silent suspicion,
the nape of my neck prickles.

I turn to bushes just outlined,
a brightening sky, clouds breaking apart,
fingernail crescent coming clear
of the fells, lifting to spotlight
the stream. The land lies bleached,
pebbles pimple the shore, the water mirror
flashes my flailing arm, casting
alarm across the pool.

ALDER-TREE

A painter would have placed it in that spot
precisely, for its mirrored symmetry,
the way it balanced the weight of the fells.

An engineer would have built his buttress
there, transforming turbulence to glide,
turning aside the gouging stream.

From roots and shade, chance made the spell
that tempted fearful sea-trout shoals
to linger, curtained from sunlight stare.

The alder-tree was picture, buttress and spell
till a storm gust tore out all it held.
Chain-saws lopped, tractors dragged the trunk,

boulders were levered, the bank made good,
but where magic was lost no fish would rest.
The alder logs lay rotting.

FEATHERS

Each morning fresh feathers on the floor
As if hens had been here secretly
Dust-bathing, scratching around,
Light Sussex, Plymouth Rock,
Rhode Island Red, identified.

Through the fifty-year-old ticking
Of inherited cushions comes
An insistent tapping till
The beak breaches the shell.

Then the duties of grain and water,
The flock half-flying towards me,
Locking at dusk against the fox,
Lifting the slide in the morning
For hen palaver down the gangplank;
The importance of gently carried eggs,

And in due season, each neck pulled
Until the bone broke sudden,
The admired knack of killing —
Though one tough old cock
Had to be chopped with a swatch
On the block by the stick-heap.
It reared headless
Staggered six or seven steps
Spouting its arch of blood —

Aprons of feathers plucked
From warm pimpled flesh,
Fingernails picking out
Ink-laden embryo quills,
The awed mystery of entrails,
The unfinished sequence in the oviduct.

I choose a red cock hackle,
Stroke back the fibres standing proud
With sheen and glint, alive.
I'll tie a fly, there's buoyancy here,
A past that I can hold
To catch a trout tomorrow.

ACID RAIN

Who killed the salmon?
I, said the Esk, with my lethal spate
I killed the salmon.

Who dripped in venom?
I, said the spruce, with my needle fangs
I killed the salmon.

Who added more poison?
I, said the rock, with my metal potion
I killed the salmon.

Who made the acid?
I, said the cloud, with my distillation
I killed the salmon.

Who corrupted the cloud?
I, said the fire, with my sulphur vapour
I killed the salmon.

And who lit the fire
demanded more power, didn't fit filters?
Who killed the salmon?

MARCH BLACKBIRDS

High-tailed on his urging tide
the usurper cock sails in
but the king intercepts, tacking
alongside, stealing the wind
stemming the flood.

Out on the ebb they go to where
new power swells again for invasion.
Five times already I have watched
their fishtail signal flags
lift and dip in undecided impasse
somewhere by the seventh bush.

And now the brown mate swoops
her fierce attack, with open beak
spread wings and claws she gamecocks
the pretender back to the fields.

But he will come again, ten times a day,
in case a cat has crunched a space,
a frontier to hold, by the seventh bush.

SEA–GULLS

As the tractor shudders into gear
they drop from an empty sky,
side-slipping gliding hovering
their snowstorm pursues the plough.

Each flake leapfrogs flutters dives
rises to follow to dive to rise,
goes into the lead to be left behind
as furrows offer easy pickings.

All day they take their tumbling turn.
At dusk they float on a tarn
anoint every feather.

A vixen sniffs the broken field,
and where a furrow sprang back green
finds the gift of two trapped gulls.

BLACK DOGS

Through the caravan curtains I expected
dawn mist smoking, Herefords grazing,
the conversational flight of greylag geese,
sheep-speckled pastures . . .

Not the flock huddled,
a white hogget separate,
rearing, held throat and haunch
in the jaws of two black dogs,

the combat frozen, an Attic vase,
growls wiped away by the wind.
Wool scattered, monstrous thistledown.
I shouted, seized a stick and ran.

The sheep lay dead. The dogs had gone,
to lie on a hearthrug licking their claws,
tonguing bright their fangs,
their faultless fangs and claws.

We point to chains and solid doors,
declare our dogs are white,
but when our dreams pick locks,
when nightmares prowl at large,

who can tell where his hounds have been?
Or where they lust to go?

ANTS

Like fell-racers at Grasmere Sports
they surge uphill, clamber round crags
climb brant out of sight to the top,

while those who have been up the spruce
gallop down double-pace, a moving belt
of bellies swollen with aphis milk.

Deep underground their queen breeds
and broods, programmes mass labour
dawn to dusk from May to September.

Daily I watch for any deviation,
eager to salute the first
free thinking ant in history.

HEDGEHOG

is shadow among shadows, night-stealer,
rustle in the shrubbery at dusk
when eyes can't be trusted,
fence-wire twanging, snuffle
heard through wide-open windows
where we lie awake with summer heat,
tracks in the dew where he drank
from the dish the starlings dowse in,
the squeeze of excrement he leaves.

SHEEP–DOG AND SHEPHERD

She was folded wings at Jack's heels,
then a blue-grey blur girdling the field,
almost before he gave the sign.
They were closer than words.

Wall-eyed, Fly was wise to divine
when a rogue sheep might jink,
which rebel was planning escape,
how far to move in to mesmerise.

Eager searcher out of sight,
gathering ewes from hidden places,
ghylls and gullies, bracken beds,
pouring the flock down the fell.

Lusting to huddle them, wolf-teeth
inheritance trained not to touch,
the predator's leap suppressed
to please him, king of the pack.

At his heels when the clod-crusher
fell. Too close to jump clear.
Now each morning by his bed
her cured pelt nudges his feet.

WICKS

Sheep-dip deters but wears away,
besides there are wounds,
a horn bleeding in its socket,
foot-rot and scour.
Blow-flies are built to find sores.

Under trees where a lame sheep lies
there's buzzing, eggs are squeezed out.
In a week the hoof is live with wicks,
and where the hoof has touched
the flank, flesh twitches.

If we come today we can clip
the blow-infested wool away,
cut into the quick, flush out maggots.
But the buzzing will be back,
we must come again tomorrow.

If we should have come last week,
there will be stench,
gaping armour of crusted skin,
quick mass of never-resting mouths,
a carrion crow in a rowan tree.

FIRETHORN

Orange flame licking every branch,
it might have served to top
the Christmas pudding, until today
the fire-eaters came to stoke themselves.
Now candelabra stems stand bare.

So soon they're feasting, as if winter
will not come this time, no need
to spare the hoard. We've lost
our picture blaze but won a close-up view
of feathers flexing, tilted tails

and out-thrust claws at touchdown, a moment's
tightrope sway, bright eyes exploring.
Young starlings wobble, dapple the branches.
Blackbirds gobble-gulp their fill,
a thrush at last comes sidling in.

The bush must be delighted – what else
are berries for? White blossom, scent to lure
intruding bees, reach forward to renewal
by way of incomplete digestion.
Firethorn invests in bird droppings.

SLOE GIN –
for Seamus Heaney

Let the first hard frost
expose the spiny twigs
reveal the bare-black fruit.

Reach through jutting thorns
for the blue-hazed sloes,
ignore the blood on your wrist.

Needle-prick to the hard stone,
watch their transfusion seep
through the gin. Each day

an agitation of the jar,
and after many days of alchemy,
decant this ruby in your glass

to taste silk-sliding fire
of frost and thorns
and bitter fruit.

MIDWINTER

Yesterday, the shortest of the year,
the land lay pinned by snow,
daggers threatened from the eaves.

Today when a blackbird perched
on a silver birch, an avalanche revealed
live catkins, their gold dust locked
in a safe that April sun will open.
They are here in midwinter,
they are measuring the days.

Birds too assess the angle of the light,
lilac roots are thermometers,
in leaf axil and feather lustre,
in the pulp of a chrysalis,
is the sure knowledge that days
grow shorter to grow longer.

Under the birch, a speck of purple,
Primula wanda pushes through,
first flower at the last of the year.

ON YOUR FARM

For William

Your father kept them, our grandfather too,
now you keep Herdwicks, and as I listen
to the morning radio I hear you say
their mutton and their wool keep you.

While you talk I am walking
through the Big Croft on an April evening.
Lucky lambs are sprinting jumping
to be King of the Castle on a hillock,
under thorn-bushes blotched with corpses,
cousins the East wind stabbed last week.
Dogs can't reach them, feast for crows.
The sun sinks sudden cold behind the fells,
a panic of recognition-calls dwindles
to warm milk silence.

Snug under my duvet, I walk your farm,
printing from an old exposure.
You touch the past with every step,
get today's mud on your boots.

CLIPPING DAY

Now, I remember the fear,
The ewe's flesh flinching
As shears neared her throat
For the first cut into the rise
Where new wool pushes off its past
In order to repeat it.

Then, I saw no shadow
While I orbited the sun,
My grandfather, who taught me
Exactly where to draw his smit mark,
'Two strokes across t'shoulders
And a pop at t'tailhead'.

All day identity was bleating
As I bundled fleeces,
Old outer enclosing inner new,
And kept my tally of the harvest
Stored in the dark loft.

On clipping day Grandfather surveyed us all,
His flock of sheep and men,
New growing under, out of old,
Predetermined shaped and wrapped
In the fleece of his mind.
He printed me with his family mark,
Proud passport in that country,
Not granted to off-comers.

I listened to uncles clipping and snipping,
Talking and turning the cycle of seasons,
The story of mating, lineage, and lineaments,
Hollins flock and Rawling yeomen;
The past teased out and meshed with new,
Making me one of the men.

At night I was reluctant
To wash off the grease of the day.
My mother smoothed soft blankets
For my masculine dreams.

The fleece was safe,
It turned the rain,
Slowly began to suffocate me.
I tore it from my throat
With radical words,
Went no more to clipping day,
Went South.

But wool clings,
I could not cast what lay behind,
Strands still holding me to visits
When wife and children met appraising eyes
That whistled up guilt to gather us in,
Tried to fold us again in the fold.

Two generations had to die
Before I could part with my blanket,
Sleep free with my wife
Under our own duvet.

HEARTHWORDS

'There are certain hearthwords which authenticate a feeling . . . '

Seamus Heaney

Your hearthword, your 'boortree',
does that and more, the naming spell
gives the thing itself
into our hands. We explore
we are in your bower.

My 'bulltree', its ancient twin,
brings warty touch, a thumbnail scratching
dark-green flesh, tang that clings,
bruised leaves on a hayfield bridle,
pungent against biting clegs.

But most of all, my hand encounters
a penknife carving a bulltree gun,
the hard white bone, its marrow pith.
Sambuca nigra, Elder, say none of this,
fail to reach where first roots feed.

ROOTCUTTER

Scrap-iron among nettles –
A wheel, the drum it used to turn,
Part of the casing
Lettered 'Gardner's Cutter'.

Jigsaw pieces that assemble
Into frozen-fingered mornings,
Cold clasping mangolds,
Arm-flailing to bring back feeling,
The East wind's knife.
How you had to heave
To start the wheel,
The pull at the guts
As the drum gouged yellow flesh
Into a willow skep.

While stirks stood
Winter prisoners on dung platforms
Bellowing their demands,
Foul-weather terms that we accepted,
Servants of our obligation,
The contract made with beasts we cage,
All a man undertakes
When he leads out the bull.

THE EEL

Schoolboy hounds splashing
along Churchyard Beck,
startled brown trout flashing
below the water-heck,

eagerly began to feel
under every ledge and rock.
My fingers touched an eel,
slimy sinuous shock.

Ignorant fear harried it
through thinwater gravel,
caulkered clogs parried it
writhing pell mell,

kicked the squirming belly out.
Wild stones thrown billet
broken bottle brute shouts
couldn't kill it.

Someone, it wasn't me,
seized a cobble found a nail
hammered the eel into a tree,
I fled the dying flail.

Guilt blocked all talking.
Each Sunday the scarred tree
shadowed my church walking,
stared into me.

II

THE BARN

(1)

Our hive, our store of August sun
for winter-cabined beasts. A good summer
was a full barn. Carts came, turned back empty,
came again, ironshod hooves struck cobbles,
a mare snorted as she charged the rising causeway,
winged shelvings swayed with the load,
wheels rattled. Then thunder, the barn floor
booming under fetlock-feathered Clydesdale feet.
A command, a practised delicate pacing to unload.
Bright prongs pierced and unpicked, ash handles
bent, they launched the bundles we embraced,
laid in a level course, crammed into corners,
trod tight. Crispness, countless swathes
of kizzened grass pricked our skin,
there was wildflower scent in our nostrils.
When our heads bumped the slates
we came down the ladder in triumph.

(2)
Winter mornings, forkfuls of hay pushed
with a hiss with a swish with a drop
down the foddergang gap – where once I overbalanced
with my childish bundle, plunged and bounced
softly under the feet of a cow.
Wet-pooled eyes gazed down, before I was gathered
to the curtain of a woman's hair.

A place to swing on ropes slung high,
to reach the rays from loopholed walls,
see into shadows. The light was soft,
the cows beneath gave up their warmth.
We climbed and clustered deep in hay,
unbuttoned young secrets, shared fears,
felt an itch but didn't understand
the sensual touch that enfolded us.

(3)
Just before Spring was the worst time,
ekeing out armfuls to wasting beasts,
protruding hipbones, staring ribs.
Shadows were darker in the emptied mewsteads.
Then, to surprise us, Winter had gone,
stirks stumbled down from their solid dung beds,
staggered drunk with light, they sniffed
backed away from green grass, didn't know
what it was. Milk cows came cautious,
tested each footstep but took the old way,
their tongues remembered. Soon milkpails
foamed fragrant with early wild flowers.

Easter was near, the dresses were ready,
hams had been boiled, there'd been a great baking,
neighbours were bidden to come to the wedding.
Women shovelled up hayseeds, swept the barn clean,
waxed the wide boards for the dancing.
Granite was bright with hurricane lamps,
fiddles were tireless, the Highland Schottische,
Gay Gordons, Veleta, and Polka. Couples
kept weaving in Eightsome Reels, bowing
and swinging, girls' feet flew through air.
The great barn grew warm for another harvest.

(4)
Oak beams, granite walls under Honister slates,
sandstone lintels from St Bees, are features now.
Wide picture-windows look to the fells where
Chernobyl festers. The byre houses Jaguars,
the cartshed's a craft shop.

The brown trout are poisoned,
the swallows don't come,
the barn is beautified and barren.

WILD STRAWBERRIES

At least that hasn't changed
the dyke-kest in the Square
where almost sixty years ago
the bigger lads bull-jumped at playtime.

One team made backs against the bank,
the others leapfrogged with lewd thrust
to straddle and collapse a weakling –
it happens sometimes with a heifer.
I was the cushion, felt every jump
as the prop's head dug my belly.

Wild strawberries grew there,
we used to thread the goosepimpled fruits
kebab fashion on a wiry grass
to make a mouthful, sweet-acid tasting.
Still there the strawberries,
the sharp tang of childhood.

THREE FLOWERS
in memory of Eva Rawling (1918-1992)

1. Crocuses
Your ashes were scattered on bare
February ground, but almost at once
Spring is your resurrection.
Up comes the snowdrop, virginal, pure,
then crocuses, cloth of gold
round the lilac trunks, display
the golden girl you were.
All gone to dust. But see
how the saffron petals spread
to cup the sun, life's warmth,
just as you opened your arms to me
at the last in your hospital bed.

2. Fritillary
meleagris, sweet honey of the fields,
blooms once again in our garden.
I cut a stem for your specimen vase,
it stands demure with downcurved head,
six petals patterned dark and paler purple,
ancient chequerboard, heraldic,
the colours slightly blurred,
like an old banner laid up in church,
a faded statement of well-worn virtues.
With modest pride it shows itself,
displays your hatchment to haunt me.

3. Cow Parsley
Anthriscus sylvestris, cow parsley
milky-ways with its million stars
the fringe of the old ditch
we both agreed should stay wild.
How you loved its Queen Anne's lace,
the delicate fronds of its fern leaf,
though it drooped if taken indoors.

Idly I crush a leaf in my fingers,

and at once we're walking close-clasped
in a London park, 1942 or 3 I think,
at last an evening pass from barracks.
You spread your mac among cow parsley,
lovingly we lay down together, the earthy
scent of bruised stems comes back,
the blaze of our bodies united.

LESSER CELANDINES

I expect them to be there
one day in March by a ditch,
enamelled gleam,
but this sudden glint

flashes first-time
walking-to-school surprise,
golden suns we used to crayon,
circle blobs with spread-out rays.

From heart-shaped leaves
they greet me, open, warm,
their bright young faces
wink away the years.

LET ME GO ...
after Saint-John Perse

"Leave off screwing the flannel in my ear,
my knees are still smarting
where you scrubbed a second time.
Let me go, I'll be late for school."

A firm hand holds and hurts,
holds him back from whip-top running,
hoop-trundling, new day staring
into the throat of a flower.

"Must you smooth out my shirt-tail,
intrude in my trousers, down the back
down the front? Don't touch me there,
let me go, I'll be late for school."

Out there, an early nest,
the pearl gleam of a blackbird's eye,
gold-ringed, the morning's aureole . . .
"Don't touch me there, let me go."

PRIVY

Enough daylight to make out the cross on the barn
where monks must have prayed, and round the yard
noseless gargoyle heads that Tudor Henry half-destroyed.
I loiter, test an ice-blistered puddle
with my boot, then hurry on past my uncle
to the cold touch of the stable-door sneck.
Whinnies ripple, starred heads turn, Clydesdales
fidget to be fed, a hoof strikes fire.

Warm reek of sweat wraps round me, acrid
sweat of work, the tang of harness that has drunk it,
hot days of harvest as I reach into a kist
and scoop up oats, a spilling measure,
soft lips slobber on my wrist, grain rattles the manger.
I step back quickly from the spray when a column of piss
cascades to the cobbles, to a steaming circle of froth,
to bubbles popping, a white-flecked spate down the runnel.
Ammonia. Skin around my nose prickles.
Another back arches, a tail cocks up, legs straddle
to break wind, then all the body, bent bow, squeezes out shit.
And afterwards, how curious the contortions, a face gurning,
whistling and whispering soft farts. How I gaze!
It could be a flower in bloom, closing to a bud
then blooming again, repeated till the spasm fades.
Redness and rudeness shrink, a final wink.
Heaped bread-roll shapes display the health
give off the heat of summer cornfields.

Next door in the byre, methane unmistakably cow,
jaws chomping, morning milking under way,
drumming of squirts in an empty pail,
foaming murmur as the level rises.
The milker leans to the cow, his head pressed
hard in her groin, He sweats in their close touching.
Roundnesses and moist breath fill the byre,
meadow scents from the tumbled fodder, I breathe abundance.

Haycocks are here too in the olive-green
of cowclap scarn, in its loose slatter.
Ammonia again but another spice,
this is a female place. Secrets are hidden
in that lower opening, behind those lips
with their strange discharges and seasonal swellings.
Calves swim out in a flood from there,
the same place piss pours from,
so near to the arsehole.
And the bull . . . and us.

Each morning the women would put us on trial,
"Have you been today?" and look towards the castor oil,
then send us to sit on the daily-scrubbed
white deal three-seater, where we used to read
cut-up pages of the Whitehaven News.
In the ancient privy, a stone head observed us,
as it once had watched monks struggling to purge
unmentionable sins, forbidden thoughts.

SCAR

Towelling after a bath I happen to notice
the scar's still there
papery-white below the knee
where he hit me with a burning stick
one Bonfire Night.
We were jealous rivals
for Miss Campbell's smile,
always competing in Class Two.

A clean well-mended scar,
cold ashes, a dead fire now.
But nightmare storm fans other embers,
I'm skidding in boots, the door's not there,
the bus breaks down, the train won't stop,
I'll miss the connection,
and why am I barefoot?

And why, last Wednesday, not in a dream,
did I cross the road to avoid you?

COLD TEA

Somewhere between armchair catnap
and waking I think I hear
"You've let your tea get cold",
reach out so as not to waste
the warmth of its making.
A white tide tips into sight
floods round my lips,
a drop overflows.

I wipe with the back of my hand
taste sweetness and sweat,
a long trek to the harvest field
wicker basket on my arm
good weight of buttered bread and cake.
In the other hand a burnished tin
swinging with every step
tea slapping and sloshing inside.

If my cousin was there
he might dare me to lift
the deep lid, to show off
a trick I couldn't explain.
Upside down as high as your head
not a drop would spill from the open tin
provided you sent your windmill arm
sailing smoothly round.

After the meal I stayed with the sheaves,
made stooks that someone straightened.
We raced the dusk and didn't notice
how straw scratches, thistles prick,
till the pattern stood complete,
then gathered round the tin,
in turn drank deep cold gulps,
wiped our mouths with the back of a hand.

RUMBUTTER

Not a jam, nor ever ordinary
though we spread it on bread for days
after the occasion, not cooked
just heated enough to blend
the Caribbean with Cumberland,
infuse the mixture with the care
a woman gave to celebration,
as she bent to see the moment
she should pour, so that it set
without sand-ripple blemish
in a silver dish specially
polished for the christening tea.
A sweet beginning, unguent,
the woman's warmth on the tongue,
hint of allowed intoxication,
internal glow, a birthday treat
repeated, notching another year,
and not quite hidden, the cinnamon
of the coming funeral feast.

Unpredictably
this stone out of the handful
chosen after hefting,
this stone slides quick flies free
isn't launched to immediate drowning,
but leaps — like a trout curvetting wild
across the lake till it strikes a wave
and plunges, the line left loose
in emptied fingers.

Like the day I climbed with cousins
zig-zag up the Bank, a summer day
when a rabbit burst out from under our feet
fright-kindled us to chase
the white scut bounding
into the wall which terrier-hot
we had to tear down, careless
where we threw the stones.

One stood on edge, wobbled, teetered,
lurched over slow, then leapt
into air bumped and bounced
the terraced riggs hurdled higher
longer arcs and we were launching more,
the stones went wild to go further,
each of us wild to send a stone
out of the field through the gate,
where all at once stood Grandfather.

That afternoon and all next day
we zig-zagged heavy up the Bank,
replaced each stone precisely
where his stick pointed.

Christmas candles quicken
the angels on their merry go round,
batons swing against brass domes
yet strangely there's no tinkling note,
the chime is lost, not in a silent void
but in headspace brimming with noise,
a tide roaring, the greedy suck
of undertow, shingle shifting.

An aid is an aid is not an aid,
boosts both desired and drowning sounds.
I finger the control, you're coming clear,
but others interject, voice over there,
countervoice nearer, group noise around
booming painful blasts beyond
the eardrum's Richter Scale and I'm
the only one not laughing.

RAMS' HEADS –
Greco-Persian, 4th century B.C.

Immediately,
the ancient bracelet sings,
the thing sings itself,
sings the hillman who made it.

Handwrought silver is rounded sheepfold,
frost-rag coats a limestone wall,
across the narrow gateway two rams' heads
stare eyeball challenge.

Cumbrian Herdwicks,
the very curve of their ammonite horns,
those regular pinched pastrymarks,
it's any autumn tupping-time
the moment before they back away
drop heads and surge into charge
clash-crunch of skulls.
The dunt of bone resounds,
they rock in recoil
again stand head to head.

The bracelet sings hill country,
more rock than grass, the flock
surviving hard weather, coiled horns
crashing across centuries.

GRANDMOTHER

I sat in silence
at the long scrubbed table
seeing again the kicking
of the new-calved cow,
the swollen udder's wince,
that first pail streaked with blood
here now in the beasemilk pudding.

We ate as in a ceremony
of which the words were lost
the ritual no longer understood.
No one smacked his lips
said that he tasted mystery.
Only Grandmother was sure
of more than frugality,
that the blood was meant to be eaten.

Only Grandmother was certain
that the last sheaf
from the last field of harvest
had to be offered
by the woman of the house
to the best cow in the byre
on Christmas Day.

Horns turned to our coming,
the glint of wet muzzles
worn chains wide-open eyes
at midwinter milking.
The chosen one tongue-wrapped her gift,
rattled the manger for more.
Around us the lift and fall of ribs
moistness of breath and fresh dung warmth,
shadows leaping the rafters,
and beyond the swathe of the hurricane lamp,
a dark corner by the foddergang.

We did not see the goddess in the corn
captured double chewed cast out
to live again in next year's fields.
We did not see in the darkest dark
a woman chained
her blood anointing seeds.

Only Grandmother glimpsed beyond the byre
the beasemilk's secret power,
prayer in the sheaf for the sun's return,
an old cry for the earth to quicken.

The same green memory still here,
clean-cut ridges, thrusting peaks,
the siren call to climb, to find
pure air, white water ropes twisting
down ghylls, jewel tarns set in moss.

A pair of buzzards velvet-finger air,
interlock their measured spirals, scan
the valley floor for grass blades moving,
white flash of rabbit scut, eye glint
of a vole, insect wings stirring.
Unease echoes in their mutual mewing.

All day it rains, all night it cannot stop,
spate roars, water-weight sluices the beck.
The river clears, perfect level for Silver Blue,
but the gravel bed is blotched
with upturned bellies, salmon corpses
tarnished with the acid flush.

I turn to the hills, climb to survey
the park's pattern, the net of walls,
river meanders, a gut swelling to estuary,
to the Solway shore where no one swims,
where man-made deathcap towers
heat up for accident.

On a ridge, ewes lift their heads,
stare for a moment. Lambs in alarm
run for solace, nuzzle for milk
that's loud with becquerels.

Ahead the peak stands clear, inviolate –
when man's metal hawk bursts in
swoops down the fell, is huge overhead,
all at once gone, before the monstrous
engine-scream rapes eardrums.

Peewits wheel panic, cry terror,
then there's the silence of fear.

BRUCE'S CAVE

Expectation races ahead
there'll be a scramble from the glen
squeeze into sucked-out space
half-light swallowed by dark,
we'll crawl with tallow candles.

But there's a door from a level path,
electric light, I stand in a tunnel
hewn out of rock, chisel-pockmarked –
could be wine cellar, air-raid shelter?

Yards of it before we curve
to a wider chamber where tide
or icemelt licked, as a cow's tongue
rasps away at a salt block.
Worn steps too, sentry-worn, lead up
to sky, a look-out post,
we're robbers, runaways, resistance
fighters, men outwith the law.
Dizzy drop to the Esk.

Not a sign of a spider, though a joker
has carved R.B. Weave that web if you will,
I'd rather see wild men spider-swinging
the cliff-face on chafed strands
first finding the cave –
long before chisels.

If we hadn't wasted days in disputing —
I had to be wary, the warriors
hadn't chosen me then — if the queen
had been less certain he believed
in that meek god of Kent, if he hadn't
been dumb at the end, too weak to praise Woden,
the corpse would have gone to the fire
in the old way of the Wulfingas.

Meantime, thanes found a fine boat, dug
a deep pit next his forbears, in sight of the sea.
The best of craftsmen made a roofed cabin
to house Raedwald, High King, Bretwalda,
while the women wept over him, royally arrayed
in the great hall, stag-sceptre by his side,
gold-pommelled sword, strong shield, bright
helmet that had over-topped hard battles.

All went awry when those Kentish monks
came to claim him — he should have been ashes
by then — they spoke in private with the queen,
she gave them leave to keep their vigil,
prayed with them, outlandish chants and prayers.
That night her cousins held the spears.
At dawn the monks had gone, the stripped body
gone, to what they call holy ground.

We had a burying without the body,
few knew the cloak covered only a pillow.
Gold and blood-garnets blind most men.
A fine purse of coins we provided, brimming
bucket of mead, to urge on the crew.
The queen at the last, set down side by side,
two silver spoons bearing strange inscriptions.
Warriors raised spear-shafts. Sand was shovelled.

No matter where the body lies, I see him
risen to Valhalla, sitting at Woden's side.

She washed him herself, looked on his limbs
for the last time. Women brought linen
new-laundered, and helped her to dress him –

all the apparel of a King armed for battle,
broad sword, beaked helmet, coat of mail,
a thick woollen cloak against the cold

of the grave. Alone she lingered over
the shoulder-clasp, touched its bright glass,
blood-drops of garnet, burning gold.

Then held the matching halves, eased them
together, married the interlocking pair,
slowly thrust home the golden pin.

ROSSLYN CHAPEL

Gargoyles glare by the door
but inside it's Garden of Eden luxuriance,
licence the laird allowed his masons
to let leaves run riot, leaves practised
by apprentices, picked from manuscript margins,
found in a hedgerow tangle
the wooded glen they walked through,
in a winter morning frost-leaf fountain
on a staircase window. Arbour for prayer
made of the land they knew.

How they must have loved sandstone,
freestone giving itself to the chisel,
every line scoop and gouge clearcut!
How the vines intertwine round columns,
how ferns cluster on capitals
oak leaves shade architraves. The ceiling
is sky and garden. There should be
blackbirds deceived into building a nest,
butterflies drawn to soak up sun
on the wide-open dog-roses.

Almost hidden, the Bible allegory
morality strip-cartoons squeezed into corners,
narrow friezes, skulls and skeletons
dancing their hellfire warning.
But in full view, coiled dragons
suck and sap the Tree of Life,
fanged monsters guard both doors,
ropes bind a man with pointed ears.
Pagan powers asleep in the stone
slipped out when the chisel freed them.

TOM RAWLING was born in 1916 on a hill sheep-farm in Ennerdale, Cumberland, and was educated at the village school and Whitehaven Grammar School before moving south to read History at University College, London. He spent the war years in the Royal Artillery, Anti-Aircraft and in the Personnel Selection Service as a psychological tester. After the war he resumed his career in teaching. For the next thirty years, he worked in primary, secondary and special schools, returning to Cumberland every year fly-fishing for sea-trout and writing articles for the specialist angling magazines in his spare time.

Upon his retirement in 1976, Tom Rawling began to write poetry, his work immediately finding its way into magazines and being heard at readings. He became involved with the Old Fire Station poetry workshop in Oxford where he met Anne Stevenson, whose encouragement led to the publication of his first pamphlet in 1978. When she left Oxford in 1979, Rawling kept the workshop going and ran it successfully for eight years, attracting such poets as Martyn Crucefix, Elizabeth Garrett, Peter Forbes, Jeremy Round, Keith Jebb, Helen Kidd and W. N. Herbert.

In 1982, Rawling's first collection of poems, *Ghosts at my Back* (O.U.P.) appeared and this was followed by *The Old Showfield* (Taxus) in 1984. His work has been widely published in a variety of magazines and anthologies including *Lines Review*, *Anglo-Welsh Review*, *The Honest Ulsterman*, *Other Poetry*, *Poetry Review*, *Arts Council Anthologies 6 & 9*, *Poetry Book Society Anthologies 1989 & 1991* and in *The Observer* when his poem 'Privy' was shortlisted in the Arvon/Observer International Poetry Competition in 1985.